sketchbook
SUSHI 6

Four Corners of Horbury

Richard Bell

Willow
Island
Editions

The Strands, Horbury Bridge, 7/9/04

I've seen the carcase of a rabbit hanging here. You could see this old mooring ring as the door handle on a medieval church or as a shackle in a dungeon.

A bond or a blessing? A snare or a sanctuary?

It's like my hometown, Horbury; I still can't decide whether it is one or the other.

Six years ago I wrote 'Around Old Horbury' as a town centre trail but when you've seen the town hall, chapels and churches you've seen only the public face of the town. You've seen its glories but not its soul: it's often to these quieter, sometimes shabbier, fringes that people come to think things out or just relax. As long ago as medieval times, the 'Second Shepherd's Play' of the Wakefield Mystery Plays acknowledged that in 'Horbury Shrogges' - the rough land around the town - you were as likely to encounter an angel as catch a sheep rustler.

I'm setting out to revisit the outer limits of the town, which - for better or worse - were such an influence on my earliest efforts as an illustrator and writer. I want to draw some of the hidden corners and, on the way, to celebrate Horbury's open air gallery of Victorian stone carving and delightful architectural details.

It's warm enough to wear shorts this afternoon but, as I sit drawing in the September sun, I find that I've got a nettle waving in the breeze by one knee, a bumblebee buzzing by the other and a wasp patrolling in front of me.

The countryside seems to have a sting in it today.

The yard-square sandstone block of the bridge that the ring is set in is pitted with drifts of ironstone pebbles. On the towpath side the stone is marked by a chiselled spot height. We are 28 metres above sea level.

Rounded capstones at the ends of the bridge prevented
tow-ropes from snagging in the days of horse-
drawn barges. A horse could be moved from one
towpath to the other without being untethered.
The iron handrail looks like a later addition.

Calder and Hebble Navigation, Horbury Bridge

This rusticated arch, in an embankment wall by the towpath, once led to a short tunnel that gave bargees access to the canal company's office in Bridge House. It was built around 1838 when this stretch of the navigation opened. Chisel marks in the stone slant diagonally from right to left, suggesting that they were cut by a mason holding a chisel in his left hand and hammer in his right. There are mason's marks on the blocks; one, the Roman numeral III, might be a guide for assembly.

Another tunnel: Coxley Beck enters the River Calder by passing under the canal and under the car park of the Bingley Arms.

Nellie the Narrowboat
1/11/04

It's such a peaceful scene at the canal basin this morning. A few of the narrowboat people are about: a man does a bit of gardening by the dockside while a woman takes her black poodle for a walk, taking her cup of coffee with her.

Two dog walkers arrive.

'Did you see that?!' I ask them, 'A kingfisher flew across and landed on one of the plant tubs over there.'

I'm trying to point it out to them when it flits across in front of 'Nellie' (the barge-style narrowboat), plops into the water opposite, then flies back to the canal, carrying a tiddler in its beak, and settles on a hawthorn branch over-hanging the water to eat it.

THE ISLAND

This place has long fascinated me. When we first moved down here, there were always hens and guinea fowl around the house. Sometimes a goat would greet you at the gate.

It hasn't been an island since 1952 when a navigable channel, which ran between the house and the Ship Inn, was filled in.

While the house has been spruced up recently, this old outbuilding, with its stone walls and flagstone roof tiles, retains its 19th century appearance.

In times of flood the river flows over the roots of the ashes and sycamores, lapping close to the wall of the house.

A cormorant flies downstream and later a white football follows it, floating down the river and disappearing under the bridge.

House of Mercy
(St Peter's Convent)
This memorial to
those who fell in
the 1914-1918 war
is probably the
only wayside shrine
in Horbury.
It stands by the
entrance lodge at
the gates of the
Convent, now
St Hilda's School.

Three *Hildoceras* ammonites on the school crest are a reminder of the Convent's connections with Whitby, where St Hilda was abbess in Anglo-Saxon times.

Lantern tower of the Convent's laundry,
now the school gym.

Rain brings the deep carving of this fine-grained sandstone memorial to life. The carved bunches glisten like ripe black grapes.

I can picture the mason carving the rounded masses, then dividing them up into leaves and fruits. The chisel marks are still crisp and fresh, mimicking the fine texture of smaller veins across the leaves.

The Reverend Charles Henry Angell had this stone erected in memory of his wife Jane who died on the 16th May 1870, aged 57.

OLIVER ROBERTS,
OF HEALEY, OSSETT,
died JANUARY 23rd 1867, AGED 54

I've noticed only one appearance of birds on
the Victorian monuments in Horbury
cemetery so I couldn't resist drawing
it: this flower basket is carved on the
headstone of Oliver Roberts (1823-1867)
of Healey, Ossett. It includes cones, oak
leaves, an acorn, a peach (?) and some
cabbage-like flowers.

The headstone of Joseph Fallas (1810-1876) is an unusual example of the tools of the trade being shown on a memorial and, for a moment, I wondered if this was a freemason's grave. It's also unusual, at least in this part of the cemetery, for the mason's name to be carved on the stone, as it is here, bottom left : 'H. FALLAS, HORBURY.'

The Fallases were in the building trade for several generations. Horbury town hall, dating from 1902, was built by Henry Fallas and son.

The headstone of William Sykes (1883-1935), founder of what would become Slazenger's sporting goods manufacturers, features cricket stumps. It originally also included bails, bat and ball, but they've been stolen.

HE PLAYED THE GAME

TO MY BELOVED BILL
W. O. SYKES

Horbury Junction

The wooden steps on the right go into the 'dark passage' across the river, directly beneath the Barnsley-bound line. The whole place shakes when a train goes over, a few feet above your head. To add to the drama, you can see the waters of the Calder through the cracks between the planks. The walls are the heavy, rivetted iron panels of the bridge, so it feels a bit like being in a corridor on board ship. Bulkhead lights only emphasise the darkness.

A jay lands in the sycamore (left), screeches, and flies off across the river, following the line. Soon two magpies perch on the railings of the bridge. A lone gull glides by. Two crows and three pigeons are next to fly across the river.

HORBURY INDUSTRIAL SOCIETY L^d N° 2 BRANCH 1897

Its facade embodies solid, dependable Victorian progress while, at the rear, in order to make the most of the corner site, it's more like the house that Jack built, with sawn-off corners and mini-extensions, built of chunkier blocks of sandstone: Victorian front, Dickensian behind.

Now Oates Interiors, this was once the no. 2 branch of the Horbury Industrial Society (later known as the Horbury Industrial Co-operative Society) built in 1897.

That reminds me of a Scottish television commercial of the 1960s: 'Mrs McGregor gets her oats at the Co-op.'

My wife Barbara remembers as a girl occasionally spending Saturday here when her mum and dad ran the branch. She found it fascinating to explore the hidden world of the stock rooms.

While so many shops of this period have suffered brutal 1960s designer treatment, and others have been marred by the necessity to fit heavy security shutters, this property has retained its impressive Victorian display windows and stepped entrance intact and unemcumbered.

Corner shops
don't come much
more wedge-
shaped than
this one (which
was also the
local post office),
recently closed,
on the junction
of Millfield Road
& Prospect Street.

I'd like to think that this Bacchus, on the keystone above the door of the Calder Vale hotel, with his splendid moustache and mutton-chop whiskers, is a portrait of the first landlord of this Victorian pub.

Stout wooden shutters on the side of the corner shop suit the building so much better than modern security blinds would.

Horbury weir (previous page) 30/11/04

As a contrast to the solid and sober (well, mostly sober) Victorian face of Horbury, this morning I needed a contrast: something wild, turbulent, free and timeless.

After all the murk we've had recently, I couldn't believe how vibrant the light was when I got to the river. I had intended to treat the tangles of vegetation and swirling foam in a very linear way but the whole point of this scene was the bright, low, winter sun; highlighting the grass on the ragged islands but throwing the banks into deep shadow.

Flood mark, 1947, Charles Street, Horbury Junction. The date has been painted out, as if obliterating the memory will prevent further flooding. Even the National Rivers Authority tells me that the (less severe) floods of November 2000 were 'unprecedented'. I think not!

Horbury Junction signalbox, overshadowed by
the motorway, drawn from the end of Green Lane.
Gulls screech, traffic roars and two vintage railway carriages, which have evidently just been in
for an overhaul at Bombardier Transportation,
trundle by between the regular passenger units.

There's wind over the patch of marsh, anglers at
the fishing lagoon.

As a boy, in the days of steam, I guess I had a yen to be an engine driver but the job of signalman fascinated me even more. It's hard to get a perspective on the Horbury Junction signalbox without straying onto the motorway embankment but this view, framed by the willows and birches of Millfield Lagoon, sums up the glorious isolation & independence that I associated with the life of a signalman.

In contrast to the view from Green Lane this angle on the box gives it something of the loneliness of a pagoda in a Chinese brush painting or on a willow pattern plate.

There's smoke and flares from a firework as I arrive at the lagoon. As I set up my umbrella and folding stool a border collie runs up to greet me sheepishly. A tall, bearded man in camouflage jacket soon follows.

'What was all that with the firework?' I ask him.

'Somebody had left a bag of rubbish and amongst some fireworks I found one that hadn't been lit so I thought that would be the safest way of disposing of it.'

'I thought there must be some explanation: I wondered if you were on gull-scaring duty!'

'No: but I do scare off the cormorants — there's one, coming in now, talk of the devil! — I'm bailiff here; I'm the one who has to try and keep the place in order and clear up the rubbish.'

Sowood Farm, 2pm 18/10/04

At the diagonally opposite end of Horbury, at Sowood Farm on the boundary with Ossett, this old tractor is a delight to draw. I prefer its form-follows-function simplicity to the plush, complacent lines of the average car. Perhaps when it was new it looked coolly mechanical but it has developed plenty of character through the knocks and bumps of life on the farm and acquired a patina through years of rough weather and hard work.

> The tractors lie about our fields; at evening
> They look like dank sea-monsters crouched
> and waiting.
> We leave them where they are and let them rust:
> "They'll molder away and be like other loam."
>   Edwin Muir, *The Horses*

Adamsford
Steps
29/3/04

Addingford Steps

Stout steel posts and tensioned cables were put in when the lane was widened. Already they've caught an 8ft block of the rock face, loosened when the bank below was cut away.

Over perhaps 100 years, miners wore the treads of these stone steps, on the south side of the railway, on their way to Hartley Bank colliery.

Addingford Cutting

sparrowhawk

Arden Court, the high-walled close of dour stone houses on Horbury bypass, was dubbed 'Colditz' when it was built and, from this perspective, that seems appropriate.

A geologist friend tells me that he was astonished at the extent of the cutting when he went through on the train recently but this impressive piece of civil engineering is largely hidden from the town. Seeing it from one end or the other, you might not guess that it is half a kilometre in length.

Stan Barstow used Addingford Steps as a way in which the characters in a couple of his novels escape the homely familiarity of their lives in the town for a wider but sometimes disturbing world beyond.

For 'Joby' these are steps into a life beyond his childhood while, in 'Just You Wait and See', Ella Palmer's walk up the steps in wartime blackout is full of looming menace.

For me, and my childhood friends, Addingford was the place we escaped to on a weekend. As an art student, I worked the day in a Polytechnic tower block, overlooking the traffic roaring through a concrete canyon in Leeds and I longed for the evening when I'd set out with my sketchbook to walk right around Addingford: past the steps, along the canal and back via the dark passage.

This was where my inspiration and my real work lay.

Riverside path, Addingford Mill, 3.55 p.m.
The light is almost gone and I hear a whispering,
whistling, wheezing behind me —
'tchou-tchouff...tchou-tchouff...tchou-tchouff...'
-like windscreen wipers on steroids. I look over my
shoulder up river to see two mute swans (the noise
is their wing-beats) looming out of the pre-sunset sky.
They go over about 15 feet above my head, white
feathers tinged pinkish gold by the evening light.
Calder valley commuters going home to roost from
their daytime haunt by the canal basin.